21 Days of Encouragement:

A Devotional

J. Scott

jackie@jackiescottartist.com

Jackie Scott
PO Box 80036, RPO Concession
Hamilton, ON L9A 0A6
www.jackiescottartist.com

21 Days of Encouragement: A Devotional / Jackie Scott, 1st Edition
Print ISBN: 978-1-7380922-4-6
eBook ISBN: 978-1-7380922-5-3

Book Cover Design: **Rebeca-Ira (through Fiverr)**

For Mum & Dad

love you lots!

Table of Contents:

J. Scott

Introduction

Couldn't we all use a little more encouragement in our lives? I sure could. It's not that we have people actively discouraging us, but sometimes no matter how much encouragement we receive, we never really believe it. We don't feel that we are worthy of encouragement, or that people must be mistaken of our value.

My hope is that this book will show everyone that we are all worthy of encouragement, and that if we're ever feeling low, there is a great source for it from the One who loves us all deeply.

So sit back and for the next 21 days, let's choose to receive encouragement in our lives. We're worth it!

Day 1: Luke 18:27

Jesus replied, "What is impossible with man is possible with God."

Think about a time you saw an illusion performed; something by a professional magician or illusionist. It seemed impossible, but what you experienced felt real. Penn and Teller are really good at slowing the process down to let us peek behind the curtain and see that these illusions are just that – illusions. Sleight of hand tricks and misdirections, caused by human hands for human eyes, making the impossible seem possible. But these are merely parlour tricks.

God truly makes the impossible possible. He gives us the small instructions and glimmers of insight that seem to come out of nowhere; the inspirations that keep us on the road to success. These are all gifts from God.

Do you think that for any moment it was possible for humans to build pyramids, construct Stonehenge, or build the Great Wall without guidance, spoken straight into the hearts of the dreamers, the architects, or the engineers? Or to inspire the workers to lift the stones heavier than were humanly possible to lift? With God, this became possible; even if they didn't know what to call him then, they knew he was there.

Even now humans are trying to solve the mystery of how these things were created with only primitive tools and without modern machines. Well, what about space flight? That is a more recent human achievement. How long was it from when Orville and Wilbur Wright first flew their plane in 1903 to when the first manned rocket left the ground for space in 1961? Less than 60 years.

Think of the leaps in human technological growth. And think of the downfalls. What else have we done since that time? Think back to the industrial revolution. What became more of a focus for humans?

Money. Wealth. Power. Possessions. More for the everyday person, to gain some of the prestige that wealthier people had. I'm not saying all of this was wrong, as everyone should have access to a good life with all they need to survive and thrive on. But what have we lost? Pastoral living, subsistence farming, the spirit of communities taking care of each other. Art. Community projects that last for thousands of years. Now it seems that our household goods, lifestyles, and even art are more disposable.

We've become so preoccupied with working for money to make ends meet in the mundane, we've forgotten that above all, God wants only our relationship with him. He wants us to love and live out the dreams he placed on our hearts. However, we think it's impossible to be that painter, poet, architect, electrician, or plumber because someone said we couldn't.

If God has put it on our heart, he will provide a way for us to achieve it. There will always be a way, if not in the timing or method we expect. But one thing must be there: we must *believe* it is possible. We must have faith. Just like the people who moved the stones heavier than any human could – they believed they could do it because they were fulfilling a purpose, doing something to honour God (in whatever format they understood him to be at that time). All of these things were possible, because of God and with God. That is what everyone forgets.

Thoughts:

What impossible thing has God put on your heart? What gifts, tools, or provision has he put in your hands to achieve it?

Day 2: Mark 10:27

Jesus looked at them and said, "With man this is impossible, but not with God; all things are possible with God."

Why wouldn't everything be possible with God? He created the universe and everything in it. Everything from stardust to molecules, to the smallest specs of minuscule particulates to the largest planets and vast galaxies. Why would anything be impossible for him? So, why do we limit what he can do through us?

We are not God, but we are all born from him in a spiritual sense. I'm starting to get it now. In Psalm 139:13 where it says "you knit me together in my mother's womb", or he knows the numbers of the hairs on your head (Matthew 10:30 paraphrased). All those miraculous things flow through and from God. He knows everyone that will come into being, and also those that will not.

He has seen everything and knows everything. We may occasionally drift off path and throw ourselves for a loop, but if we start to stray too far, we feel this divine nudge guiding us back on course.

For example, here I am writing another book. I loved writing and stories as a child, but somewhere along the way I got discouraged or distracted, and never believed I would write a book, let alone publish one. I doubted myself and the gifts God gave me, until I saw a post about a free workshop on how to outline a book. I attended the workshop and it turns out I really did have the words in me after all, I just kept denying it — or avoiding it — or never considered it was possible for me. I had forgotten that "everything is possible with God," until I was reminded of that truth. So now here I am reminding you.

He has a plan for us, but it is still up to us to step into it. He sets the course for our lives, but it is our responsibility to live it. I think that is why humans are so dear to God, and why we've exasperated him since the Garden of Eden.

He provides us with all we will ever need, with life, creativity, all the raw materials and sustenance we could ever want, and what do we do with it? We say "nope — we can do better!" We start striving and fighting against nature, both in the world and in ourselves. We build bigger and dirtier things that strip the planet of its resources, that cause havoc and destruction. We leave behind a legacy of plastics and toxins. Then we fight over these same things, using bombs, guns, bullets and things not from God to destroy flesh, nature, and human creations. Why? To see who has the most power? The most stuff? The most control?

None of that matters one bit.

God has all the power, control, and something even more powerful – the LOVE.

What more could we ask for than God's love and peace in our lives? From that we can do all and we can be all that he has planned for us. Why?

Because *everything is possible with God*.

We have to stop relying on ourselves. We have to stop isolating ourselves from the One who created everything. He knows our very souls and hearts anyway, so why bother fighting it?

Thoughts:

Let the love in. Let the peace in. Let God's love, peace, and provision flow in your life. Receive the truth that you are loved by God, that we are all loved by God. We all have this amazing love flowing through us, and this love connects us all. From that, peace will come. We need to be brave and lay down guns, and reach out our arms to embrace one another in peace and love. Because everything is possible with God. Even world peace, if we win over one person at a time. Amen!

Day 3: Mark 9:23

"What do you mean, 'If I can'?" Jesus asked. "Anything is possible if a person believes."

What do you believe you can do?

Do you believe you can write an opera? Tend a garden? Make that dress? Paint those pictures? Write those books? Make those pots?

If you believe it, it is possible. Because anything is possible if a person believes.

That doesn't mean that it will automatically happen, that it will suddenly appear in front of you complete, like a wish granted from a genie in a bottle. It means that your desire and your belief will see you through the long hours spent gaining the skills to live your dream.

Nothing happens without effort, and I love the quote where David says he will not give to God that which cost him nothing (1 Chronicles 21:24, paraphrased). Achieving what you believe requires effort. It requires time spent trying, failing (or what I consider learning), and trying again.

Why do I consider failing learning? Because I always learn more from those things which don't succeed than I learn from things that work the first time I try them. For example, teapots. These are probably one of the trickiest forms to make as a potter, because it requires the body, the lid, the spout, and the handle all to be at the right temperature (or drying stage) at the right time to assemble it without any cracks. Each part has its own skill level to achieve, and its own tricks. Does the lid fit the body? Make two of them just in case. Spout? How do you want it to sit? What kind of shape? How will you construct it? What kind of handle(s) or connections will you use? What kind of shape? Will it be too big, too thin, or too awkward? Even if you end up getting the construction right, what about the glazing? Will that turn out? I have a wonderful collection of imperfect teapots on my shelf. Each one has an awkward thing about it, but I love each of them for what I learned from them.

No matter how many I make I keep trying, because I learn something each time, even though it's not what I really want to create. I can't help myself. This last teapot I made a few days before writing this entry is the largest I've made. So far it seems to be okay, but one can never tell until it's all the way through the firing process. But I believe I can make it again if I need to. (Note: I can happily report that it made it through the whole process intact, and pours like a dream! You can see a picture at jackiescottartist.com).

I also believe I can write. God has given me years of experience writing, and has given each of us a unique perspective on his Word, which may reach others and inspire or encourage them, so I want to share it. And that's coming from a confirmed introvert who would happily remain a nameless, invisible hermit. If God has other plans for me, I'll defer to him because he knows better than I do.

Thoughts:

What is on your heart? Trust that God put it there for a reason. Believe that God put it there for your good. Believe that you can achieve it, because "Anything is possible if you believe."

I believe you can, because God can do all things. Amen!

Day 4: Philippians 4:13

For I can do everything through Christ, who gives me strength.

This has been my mantra since I first read it in 2011. It's hard to believe it's been that long, and yet it hardly seems like it's been anytime at all. It also feels like I've known this truth forever.

Anxiety has been my constant companion for as long as I can remember, until this verse replaced it. Since I've adopted this verse, I've gone from a total introvert to someone who has:

• faced her fear and sung aloud in church, then as a part of the worship team, then as a back-up singer in a band at a fundraiser, and solo at a memorial for a dear friend

• gone away overnight on my own a couple of times (I don't travel well)

• completed my Anthropology degree and walked across the stage at my convocation with confidence (and without being ill from nerves)

• written a few worship songs, recorded a few of them as demos at the legendary Grant Avenue Studios, and even performed a couple of them live at church. One of them was even streamed over the internet in one of our last worship services before our church closed down in 2021

• participated in the local pottery guild mentorship and exhibition, the 50th anniversary guild exhibition, had a piece in their juried biennial exhibition in 2024, and participated in one of their local sales

• self-published three devotionals (and counting!)

• and most importantly, I've married the most wonderful man, the love of my life, who encourages me in all my artistic pursuits. Okay, that happened before I found my way back to God, but I'm very grateful that God blessed me with such a wonderful man in my life.

This may not seem like much to some people, but when you remember that I am an introvert and have battled with anxiety my whole life, any one of these achievements would have been amazing. Here I am now, writing devotionals to encourage others, because with God, all things are possible, and that includes living a full and blessed life, regardless of what life throws at you.

We *can* do all things through Christ who strengthens us.

It is not by my own power or my own blessing that I did any of these things. When I tried to do any of these on my own, they did not succeed. Honestly, I wouldn't even try. I would be overwhelmed and not even start. But that is not the case now.

Okay, there are still some days where fear grips me, but I will not let it win anymore.

God is with me. He is with you, too. He wants us to succeed and to achieve the goals he has placed upon our hearts. That's why we're here. He will always provide for us, and he will give us all we could ever need or want. We are all blessed by him, and should honour him – not with sacrifices, but with living our dreams. I suppose that is a sort of sacrifice; we are sacrificing our fears to achieve that which he has blessed us with.

Prayer:

Do not be afraid. Do not give up. When the enemy comes calling, pull out this cloak of strength and wrap it around you. Be that which you were born to be:

Artist.

Musician.

Welder.

Draftsperson.

Architect.

Accountant.

Mother.

Father.

Poet.

Friend.

Any number of dreams upon billions of hearts. They are all possible. Because we *can* do all things through Christ who strengthens us.

Amen!

Day 5: Isaiah 41:10

Don't be afraid, for I am with you.
Don't be discouraged, for I am your God.
I will strengthen you and help you.
I will hold you up with my victorious right hand.

Fear and discouragement often go together. It is so much easier to be discouraged when we feel afraid. It is so much easier to be afraid when we are discouraged. It's kind of like bacon and eggs, Laurel and Hardy, peanut butter and jam, or any other pairing here that makes sense to you.

What we may not be used to, is encouragement. "Don't be afraid, for I am with you. Don't be discouraged for I am your God. I will strengthen you and help you."

It seems so simple! Why wouldn't it be simple? God is with us. He is our God. He will strengthen us and help us. We are not alone. We do not have to be afraid or discouraged; God's got this!

It seems so easy that I could stop writing here, but I find we often need more convincing.

"Really? How could this possibly be true? How could God possibly be everywhere at once? Why would he care if I am afraid or discouraged? No one else cares!"

That can be what it feels like when we're being beaten down by the world, everyone is mean to us ,and it feels like we have no hope.

There is *always* hope.

There is *always* a way.

Jesus.

God made a way for us through Jesus, and through Jesus, God is with us. He is everywhere at once, because he's God. He's not human. He's not limited like us. He will never leave us or lead us astray. God is our cheerleader, our best and most loyal fan; our soft shoulder to cry on when we feel all alone, and our dearest Father, who will pick us up, dust off the dirt, and set us on our feet again when we've fallen down.

God cares for us. He loves us. God has known us since before we existed, and will know us forever. You don't invest that much time in someone you don't like. Think about it: as humans, there are some people we wouldn't even want to spend an elevator trip with. We may find them irritating or quirky and not know how to communicate with them.

Not a problem for God. He doesn't have our limited insight or vision. He sees the good in all of us, and strengthens us.

Are there terrible, horrible people in this world? Yes; or maybe they are people who have done terrible, horrible things. Maybe they've been abused, misused, and led astray. I cannot answer for them. I know there are things I'm not proud of, things I've said or done and wished I'd reacted or behaved differently. The enemy is real and very sneaky, and willing to waylay us on our path.

But God is on our side, in our corner, cheering us on, strengthening us. He is our help in times of need, and he will *always* be there for us, no matter what.

Thoughts:

No matter how young or how old we are, how good or how bad we may act, God is always there to help us, to redeem us, to correct our path if we go astray.

Do not be afraid.

Do not be discouraged.

God is with us. Amen!

Day 6: Joshua 1:9

Joshua 1:9 This is my command—be strong and courageous! Do not be afraid or discouraged. For the Lord your God is with you wherever you go."

Yesterday's entry also essentially said "Do not be afraid...do not be discouraged." Throughout the Bible God's words are often repeated to us. Why?

Because we're human. We forget quickly and are easily distracted. This is most true when it comes to our basic animal instincts like fear and panic, or when we are discouraged. Why is it so easy for us to be negative?

Why is it easier to walk down a hill or flow downstream on a raging river than it is to climb up a hill or swim upstream? Well, because it's easier. The same can be said for our mindset. It is so much easier to go down familiar negative pathways in our mind than it is to forge newer, more positive ones.

Guess what? It's not hard for God. He showed us how to follow the paths made by animals to scale higher into the mountains. He taught us how to build boats to flow upstream against the current to reach different locations we couldn't reach before.

He shows us how to not be afraid or discouraged, by having faith that he is with us wherever we go.

We are not in this alone. We are not abandoned. We are not fighting these monsters or enemies without assistance. God is with us, and good news! God always wins.

True, the win may not be the way or when we expect it. Life is lived not according to our own whims and timelines, but by those much greater than we can perceive. That doesn't mean we're like a twig swirling alone in a whirlpool, lost in the forces of nature. We're a lamb safe in the arms of our shepherd. We're a child on our Father's lap, or in our Mother's arms. We will not be harmed while God is with us (which is always).

Bad things happen to people all the time, but we do not have to wallow in them. I read a quote today: "Pain is inevitable; suffering is optional" (attributed to the Dalai Lama among others). We can rise above any challenge, defeat any fear or foe, and win the battle. God is with us.

Do not be afraid! Do not be discouraged! All things will come together for good, even if it doesn't seem like it now. Maybe we lost that job so we'd get that kick in the pants to live out our dream. What's the worst thing that can happen if we're already at rock bottom?

Prayer:

Trust God. Really! He's got this! Know that he means the best for us in our lives. Trust that he wants the best for you, and that he is with you, carrying the heavy gear to lighten your load as you climb this mountain in life.

Don't give up. Keep going. The view from the top of your mountain will be spectacular!

Trust in him.

Do not be afraid.

Do not be discouraged.

God is with you, always. Amen!

Day 7: 1 Thessalonians 5:11

So encourage each other and build each other up,
just as you are already doing.

As I'm writing this verse, there is a lovely bird singing outside my window. A chorus of them, actually: a robin, a mourning dove, several other small songbirds chirping and sharing their songs with the world. Okay; they're trying to attract their mate in springtime, but it is still beautiful to hear. Who's to say that some of the songs and conversations they have aren't to encourage each other?

In our modern world we've forgotten how to apply this verse in our lives. For so long we've been told to be the best, to compete for this or that job, to try harder. We all lose living that way. Either we feel like we've been stomped on by those who've climbed over us on the way to the top, or we may feel left behind because we chose not to enter the race.

But then you find your people and the world shifts a little. For example, I started taking pottery courses regularly in 2007. The class was made up of people from all levels, from beginners to seasoned potters, all there to learn from the instructor and each another. Even if we had pieces we weren't sure of, our classmates would point out the positives or suggest alternative ways to fix what we didn't like, showing that a community accomplishes more by encouraging one another than we'd ever accomplish tearing each other down. I've found most of the clay community is like that.

My husband also experiences this in his community of drummers. They all encourage one another, share tips, techniques, stories, and encouragement. Many artists and creatives I've met are like this. Why? I'm not really sure. Maybe it's because when we're being creative we are so much closer in our hearts to God, whether we realize it or not. After all, "In the beginning, God created..." (Genesis 1:1).

God is creator above all. Creating was his first act. Whether we are people of faith, agnostic or even atheists, creating is an act after God's own heart.

Encouragement is lacking in most areas of our modern lives. Social media is often built on polished looks and the illusion of perfection, rather than people showing their honest truths and struggles. It is so easy to give an encouraging word and to lift one another up rather than tearing each other down. Why choose to be mean? What would it be like if we reframed harsh criticisms in a positive way? What if we examined why we were being negative instead of lashing out? What if we slowed down our responses, accepted and loved each person for their own capabilities, and lifted each other up? Would negativity become a thing of the past? Probably not overnight, but we could hope.

Action Item:

Try this today: pick one or two people who have encouraged you in the past, and remember how it made you feel. Write that down. As you go about your day, try to share an encouraging smile, word, or help someone you come across. They could be a friend, family member, or even a random person. See how it feels to share God's encouragement, even with simply a smile. Amen!

Day 8: 2 Corinthians 12:9

Each time he said, "My grace is all you need. My power works best in weakness." So now I am glad to boast about my weaknesses, so that the power of Christ can work through me.

I really appreciate this verse. I should write this down and paste it to my wall, so when I need it, it's right in front of me. Do you ever feel the same way?

For example, I've struggled for years with migraines. From my teens to my late twenties, I didn't even know what they were, I just knew that my head would hurt, my body would ache, and I'd feel queasy. I would power through thinking "it's just a headache."

Then after a particularly painful headache one night, I woke up the next morning with a numb left foot. I thought I slept wrong, but throughout the day it got worse. A trip to my new doctor resulted in him telling me it was a migraine. Several specialists and many tests confirmed his diagnosis. I have a type of migraine that starts in the head then migrates into one side of my body, so my body aches instead of my head. I like to think that's a coping mechanism my brain implemented from ignoring the headaches for so long.

What I didn't realize was that this pain was making me miserable. I was cranky and sarcastic to those closest to me; my parents, siblings, friends, and eventually my husband. I did not realize that I was taking my pain out on them for decades; we all thought I was just like that. I only recently realized that the pain my body was feeling was affecting my mood and making me a cranky, sarcastic, and generally not-fun-to-be-around person.

Now I know, however. How could I change my mood and the way my pain affects others?

"My power works best in weakness."

I had to admit that I was in pain, and that no matter what I tried, that was the reality I was living. *Is* the reality, actually. I have two choices. I can continue trying to fight the pain and be a mean, cantankerous soul to everyone I know, or I can pause, acknowledge the pain, and let God take over where I cannot.

So, while I'm waiting for another specialists referral, I've been going to physiotherapy and acupuncture to help alleviate the symptoms, as the different medications either didn't work well or were too strong for me. I'm eating better, resting better, and taking better care of myself. When I'm having a particularly bad day physically, I rest. I don't try to push through or force myself to power through my pain anymore. Please note: this is not medical advice; I'm merely recounting my own story.

Why this change?

Because I decided to let myself receive grace. I decided to accept my physical weakness not as something debilitating, but as a way to let God work in my life. I've found a way, by receiving God's grace and letting his power carry me where I cannot carry myself.

I am kinder to myself and not angry with my body for being the way it is (well, not *as* angry.) I am letting myself receive God's grace, recognizing that while I may look fine to others on the outside, I have to accept my limitations, give them to Jesus, and let him show me how to live within them.

Maybe you've experienced something similar, where you struggle with some form of pain whether physical or emotional, and it affects how you interact with others. Maybe it causes you to be sarcastic and bitter, or withdrawn and reserved. It doesn't have to be that way.

We don't have to let our pain change our spirit. Trust God, and release your pain to him. Let yourself acknowledge it, and trust that God will use it for good.

Thoughts:

Trust God. Do not be afraid or discouraged. His grace is all we need. His power works best in our weakness. Why would we think we can do it all? Surrender to God, who *can* do it all, heals all that ails us, pains us, causes us fear and anger. Let him guide us from there. Amen!

Day 9: Philippians 4:6

Don't worry about anything; instead, pray about everything. Tell God what you need, and thank him for all he has done.

When do we usually need the most encouragement? When we are worried. That's when the "it's okay; it will all be good; everything will turn out okay" cheerleaders usually come out to encourage us. Here is a great guide to follow when we're worried or concerned about something:

"Don't worry about anything." Yeah, easier said than done. How do I do that?

"Instead, pray about everything." That's all well and good, but what do I pray about? How do I pray?

"Tell God what you need, and thank him for all he has done." Oh! That seems easy enough!

Too often we make things more complicated than we need to. We try to come up with complex prayers or forget that the easiest way to calm down when we're flustered is to stop, pause, breathe, and pray. We often can't get to the "stop and pause" part, let alone the "breathe and pray," and I'm one of the worst offenders.

It's usually technology that frustrates me, and I'm fairly technologically adept; well, at least I eventually stumble across the right way to do something. Then I'll try to replicate it, and either can't quite remember how I did it the first time, or the systems were updated and I have to figure out the new way and carve a new neural pathway to complete the same task I did last week.

That's tricky when it's not something you do often. Or I come up with something I want to communicate, but the computer programs won't do what I want. I'll try to figure out something by looking on Google for the answer, or checking out another technique on YouTube, and then it still doesn't work. At that point, my frustration level increases. Early in my career that was easier; you could smack the side of the CRT monitor or the desktop computer and feel better about it. Now the temptation to hurl a laptop across the room is too expensive an option, so instead it's time for a break.

Go for a short walk; pause; breathe and pray. Okay, at work when I'm frustrated I'm usually not praying, but something similar happens. As I walk, my mind frees up, and frustration ebbs. Once that happens, then my mind can freely work the problem. I walk through the steps and various options, and the solution usually presents itself.

Then some relaxed conversational prayers start flowing, too.

That is the same effect prayer has on other situations. There is the old adage of counting to ten before you get angry or say anything in anger. Not sure I've ever employed that myself; I've always been terribly quick with a sarcastic response. A quick wit, sarcasm and sense of humour are a terrible combination when it comes to trying to be patient.

But that's the calming presence of Jesus. As you focus on something other than what you're getting frustrated or worried about, you calm down. Adding prayer allows you to rest, to focus on things that are more important, thanking God for what he has done: "Thank you for providing me with this job, Lord." Tell him what you need: "I can't quite figure this out – if only I knew how or could ask so-and-so …Hey! Why don't I ask this person?" And oftentimes, just like that, he will provide the solution by letting us clear away the clutter in front of it.

Thank you, Lord, for always providing a solution! Amen!

Action Item:

Try this technique once or twice this week when you are beginning to feel worried, frustrated, or overwhelmed.

Stop.

Pause.

Breathe, and pray.

Journal about the results, and then try it again.

Day 10: Philippians 4:7

Then you will experience God's peace, which exceeds anything we can understand. His peace will guard your hearts and minds as you live in Christ Jesus.

This is a continuation of yesterday's verse about not worrying about anything, but praying about everything. "God's peace, which exceeds anything we can understand." Or "The peace of God, which transcends all understanding, will guard your hearts and your minds in Christ Jesus." (NIV)

Peace that "exceeds anything we can understand" or "transcends all understanding." I love that! How encouraging is it that we can have peace; peace that soothes and calms our souls, our hearts, our minds. And all we need to do to receive it is to pray about anything and everything. Simple conversations in our hearts and minds with our Heavenly Father, with Jesus, and with the Holy Spirit. We didn't have that as an option for this peace before Jesus. Jesus made us whole with God, by being the sacrifice for all of us.

Humans are flawed. It's not our fault, it's how we were made. God realized this, and he provided a solution. In a very 21st century tech-y way, God supplied Jesus as the software patch to our faulty operating systems. We were good until we listened to the serpent — or any other manner of origin story for those from different faiths. The solution is Jesus.

He chose to live and die so that we would receive this peace that goes beyond all understanding, so that we would have this relationship with God, our Heavenly Father, through Jesus' love and sacrifice. Jesus rose again to prove to us that this was true.

Yes, people have twisted and corrupted Jesus' message over the 2000 years since he walked the earth. They've used it to abuse others, to murder, rape, subjugate, steal, destroy; to gain power, wealth, and all manner of earthly things. They don't get it. They never did.

Jesus is not here for power, for dominance, for wealth, or for profit.

Jesus is here for love, for peace, for grace, and for mercy.

He came to heal the sick, to calm our fears, to bring us peace, and above all to show us that love is the answer. Love God, love everybody. And that means everybody no matter who they are, what they wear, what they believe. No matter if their politics are the same as yours or different; heck, if they're good politicians or the untrustworthy ones we seem to get, we should love them all the same. Loving someone is not the same thing as trusting someone. Jesus isn't asking us to be foolish, but to love others despite their failings — and our own.

Without love, there is no answer. So that's how it works.

Love God. Love everybody. Thank God, pray to him about everything, and you really will feel this peace that transcends everything. How do I know? I am one of the lost sheep who was found, and have walked this path in love. And I've felt this peace, which for an anxious person like me, has changed my life.

Do I still have bad days where I get angry at others? You bet. I only have to watch the news and I get fired up all over again. But then I remember: Love God, love everyone. God's got this. Share love, and breathe.

Action Item:

Take a few moments now to pause, think about what might be nagging at you or causing you some stress, and pray to God about it. Just start talking to him; tell him your fears and concerns. Release this burden to him, and receive his peace. Journal about it, and do it again tomorrow.

Day 11: Hebrews 10:24

Let us think of ways to motivate one another to acts of love and good works.

This is where community comes into play.

You may have a very small circle of friends and acquaintances or a large group. You may live in a small town, medium sized one, or a large city. Either way, there are people you will likely come into contact with frequently.

How do your interactions affect them? Are you being positive and encouraging towards them? Are you always negative, complaining about others? Is there a balance somewhere in between?

Somedays I think I do a pretty decent job of being a positive person around others. Other days, not so much. On those days I try to sequester myself if possible, so my negativity doesn't catch on to others. I suppose it's not the best way to do things, but I prefer to not spread negativity if I can help it. I'm too easily drawn down the "misery loves company" road, where pity parties are stretched out for hours on end. It's exhausting and draining. Have you ever had the same experience?

The flip side though is to mindfully move something negative into something positive. Note the mindfully part; not being mindlessly flippant about something, but consciously deciding to move from a negative moment to a positive one. We can react how we always have in the past, carelessly using the first negative phrases that come to mind, or we can mindfully pause, be patient, and grow in positivity. Will it be easy? No. Will it be difficult? At first, yes, but everything gets easier with practice.

I'm also not advocating to ignore pain, whether physical, psychological, spiritual, or emotional. I am advocating the decision not to wallow in it. Hal Elrod, the author of the Miracle Morning, has a five minute rule. If something bad happens, you can soak in it for five minutes, but after that you have to move on. It isn't doing any good for anyone to dwell on it. And he has been through a lot. You can check out Hal's story at: miraclemorning.com. I haven't fully adopted that philosophy yet, but I'm getting better at it.

What this verse suggests we do is to encourage each other to be positive, to be cheerleaders for each other.

Have you ever noticed when you encourage someone else, even if you're having a bad day yourself, you feel better? It's not to say you ignore how you feel or what you might be going through, but by sharing positivity, hope, and encouragement, something subtle shifts in our life. It's like our centre of power shifts from focusing on whatever negativity we might be experiencing to sharing positivity, even if only in a small way.

It could be as simple as smiling at someone, holding a door for someone, helping out with a clean-up day at work, or any number of simple things. It's amazing what can be achieved when we share God's encouragement with one another. Amen!

Action Item:

Write down three encouraging acts of kindness you could easily do in the next couple of days. Some ideas: smile at someone; hold a door for someone; let someone in before you in traffic; give someone an encouraging compliment. Then give one or two of them a try. How does it feel? Journal about it and track the progress of your positivity. You may have small setbacks, and that is okay. Every step forward is a step in the right direction.

Day 12: Deuteronomy 31:8

Do not be afraid or discouraged, for the Lord will personally go ahead of you. He will be with you; he will neither fail you nor abandon you.

Wow. I kept reading this verse slowly before I started writing, and it felt like this warm blanket came down and covered my shoulders, or like a warm hug settled on to me. It was like hearing someone saying "it's all going to be okay, no need to worry." It felt like drinking a cup of warm cocoa or tea, feeling the warmth spread through my body as I drank the warm liquid.

The other thought I had was "where has this verse been all my life?" I've read it before, but it hasn't affected me quite so strongly. "Do not be afraid or discouraged, for the LORD will personally go ahead of you. He will be with you; he will neither fail you nor abandon you."

Just wow. "Will personally go ahead of you;" he's not sending angels to do the work, he's on it himself! Doesn't that make you feel special?

It's like when you go to a boutique hair salon and the owner decides to do your hair personally rather than leaving it to their assistants. Or the head lawyer at a firm decides to take your case. Or the lead singer of your favourite band takes the time to personally respond to you or talk to you at a meet and greet. Think about it for a moment.

God will personally go ahead of us, clearing any obstacles out of our way, guiding us to our destination, leading us. "He will not fail you nor abandon you." He is in it for the long haul and with us always, taking care of us, guiding us, loving us, providing for us. How amazing!

It reminds me of driving home from the theatre the night before I wrote this entry. My husband Michael was playing in the orchestra pit band for a local student theatre production and I went to see the play. It ended late at night —quite late at night for me — and I was driving myself home. I was a little anxious because I had recently heard lots of stories of terrible car accidents, and that kept playing in the back of my mind. The enemy likes to take advantage of those moments when he can, but I remembered that no matter what, God was with me and all would be well.

Even though I wasn't very familiar with the area I was in, I knew I wouldn't be lost, that God was with me, and I would always find my way home. Although there was still that quiet negative voice in the back of my mind, I let God's word and presence surround and protect me, and all was well.

It may seem silly, but sometimes small things can be big challenges. And they are always worth it, as long as God is at the heart of what you do. I went there to encourage my husband, and no amount of negative self talk was going to keep me from being there and safely making it home. Love is always more important than fear. God is love, and he is everywhere. Sometimes we just have to believe.

Have you ever experienced something like that before? Where you were afraid to go and do something because of negative self-talk or a nagging fear? Use this verse as the encouragement to help you overcome any fears or negativity. Embrace the amazing life that God has planned for you. You won't regret it!

Prayer:

Heavenly Father, thank you for being with us through all the days of our lives; the good moments, the challenging ones, the amazing ones. Thank you for blessing us with your peace, your love, your kindness, your grace, your mercy. May your love spread through all the world, as we remember we are all your dearly loved children. In Jesus' name I pray, Amen!

Day 13: Psalms 56:3

But when I am afraid, I will put my trust in you.

How do I even begin this one? With a memory.

Lauren Daigle has a song called "Trust in You." It was the battle cry for a friend of ours as she fought breast cancer. Sadly it was a battle she lost. We sang it for her in her hospital room a couple of days before she went home to be with the Lord. She didn't have the strength to talk, but she did squeeze each of our hands in turn, trying to encourage us as we feared and mourned losing her.

We sang it again at her celebration of life, and I sang it again in honour of her later that evening as the memorial turned into a celebration concert with her family and friends. It was the first time I'd sung solo in front of a crowd of people who weren't from our church. I was afraid of not having her around anymore, of singing in front of a crowd and of so many other things, but I trusted in God, and I made it through.

I'm even a little afraid this morning, as I'm going away overnight for a couple of nights by myself to a women's retreat. I've been looking forward to this for a while, but still, old anxieties like to creep up every so often. I know I have nothing to fear, because God is with me.

Our friend knew she had nothing to fear as she squeezed our hands. Her faith was incredible to behold. She had faith beyond measure, and kindly shared it with everyone she met. She did so even more boldly when she knew that her time on earth was limited. She shared it with doctors, nurses, patients who needed encouragement, and everyone who was tired or fearful or frustrated.

She leaned deeply on her faith. No one wants to die. She loved her family fiercely and did not want to leave them, but she also knew with all her heart she was going home to the arms of Jesus, welcomed with an embrace and all the love in the universe. She would have answers to all the questions she ever had. She would be in the presence of her saviour. She was encouraging us to the very end.

She encourages us even now. Every time I see a hawk I think of her (they're fairly rare in our area, or at least they used to be). I feel like it's her flying free and encouraging me, simply by flying by or resting on a lamp post as I drive past.

God works that way in our lives. He is always there for us, even if we don't know it. Even if we never thought of it before, we could probably pick out a time we were frightened yet still moved forward in faith, and felt an unexplained wave of calm that blanketed us. It may not have seeped deep into our soul; we may still have had shivers of fear, but we walked through that fear and did it anyway. "But when I am afraid, I will put my trust in you."

Do not put your trust in the things of this earth. Buildings crumble. Weather changes. People are notoriously unreliable. God is unchanging. He is the same yesterday, today, and tomorrow. He is reliable, and we can trust in him.

Thoughts:

He loves us so much he sent Jesus to ransom us, to pay for our sins, because rather than destroying us, he wanted us to come back to relationship with him. Receiving this gracious gift of salvation and relationship. Love God, love others, and restore this world to what it should be. I choose to trust in you, God! Thank you, Jesus!

Day 14: Galatians 5:14

For the whole law can be summed up in this one command: "Love your neighbor as yourself."

I always thought this was a complicated quote, because I knew a lot of people who treated themselves worse than anyone else around them. How can we love our neighbours as we love ourselves, when we're not even sure we *like* ourselves? Easy!

Remember that God loved us first.

Really? How on earth is that supposed to help? Aren't I supposed to be chasing it all? Climbing the corporate ladder? Dog eat dog? To heck with the next person? Or how is there even time to learn to love ourselves when we've never had the time to pause, listen, and even learn who we are? We're busy running from this activity to the next, working through school and work. Between chasing activities and binge watching shows or playing video games to decompress, we don't slow down enough to even realize what our favourite colour is.

How can we love ourselves if we don't even know if we *like* ourselves?

Pause. Breathe. Relax. We can love ourselves, knowing that God loves us. God loves each of us, individually, and wholly, just as we are. He knows us deeply, all our plusses and minuses, our positives and where we lack. He knows our soul, deeper than we do. And he loves us no matter what. He even likes us.

Love and like are two very different things. Take families for example. We're born into a family and we have no choice over it. We love our parents, siblings, aunts, uncles, cousins etc. no matter what, flaws and all, because they are family. We may not like them very much — the cheek pinchers, the squishy huggers, the hermits we rarely see; the alcoholics, the violent or angry ones, or the criminals. But we still love them because they are family. So in families, we love each other because of that familial bond. God is the anchor to all humans – all creation, really – because he loves the birds in the sky and insects on the ground as well as he loves us.

That brings me back to loving ourselves. We need to have more grace for ourselves, remembering that God loves us. We have to stop trying to be validated by the love of other people – partners, family, friends, coworkers – and remember that we are enough, just as we are. Receive God's love into our hearts, just as we are, where we are at today.

When we do that this wonderful thing happens. We start to like ourselves a little more. We have a little more grace, a little more patience, and we take a little bit more care with how we talk to ourselves. Then we start doing the same with those around us. We pause and are more patient when someone does something we don't agree with. We are kinder and more understanding. We hold the door open for a stranger. We let others go first in line even if they have more things. We pause, and count to ten before responding when someone is mean, remembering that we do not know what they are struggling with.

And with that, God's love flows through us to those around us. That is how we love ourselves, and then, we love our neighbours.

Action Item:

Receive God's love in your heart. You are worthy just as you are. Share this amazing unconditional love with yourself, and then start sharing it with others. Try picking one kind and encouraging thing to say to yourself today, and repeat it each day for a month. See how that helps change your perspective.

Day 15: John 1:4-5

The Word gave life to everything that was created, and his life brought light to everyone. The light shines in the darkness, and the darkness can never extinguish it.

The Gospel of John begins with such poetry as he talks about the Word. This is another term for Jesus, as John describes the Word as a person, its own entity although part of God. I'm still learning so I don't understand that too deeply yet. It took me listening to one of the children's Bible school stories to understand the Trinity of God, where they described it like an egg. The whole egg is God, with its three separate parts (yolk, white, and shell) being the three parts of God (God, Jesus, Holy Spirit respectively). I probably got the order wrong, but hopefully you get the gist of it. Maybe the Word is meant to be the translation of God to humans. Jesus taught the existing scriptures to people because he understood them so well; he was the Word, so he could translate the true meaning to us.

What I want to focus on is light. Light shining in the darkness. Light that can never be extinguished. It is so beautiful. I suppose it is hard to think of true darkness now, at least where I live in a highly populated city. Lights are everywhere, and even at night blackout curtains are needed to keep out most of the streetlight's glow to try and get a good sleep. I can walk through my house at night without turning on a lamp because there is enough ambient light that no room is ever truly dark.

That's like Jesus. He's light through the darkest spaces and moments in our life, so we can always find a way out. I imagine that the night would be much darker in rural areas, where there are fewer houses grouped together. But then the moon and stars are there to light the way. Even on a cloudy night the clouds would reflect what little light is there to give some comfort and brightness.

"His life brought light to everyone." No one is left out. It doesn't say "he brought light to this or that group" or "everyone except …" Jesus' light was brought to everyone.

There is so much division in our world today, so much "us against them," competition, political division, and more people twisting the truth than ever before. That was not and is not God's plan for the world.

He does not divide. He does not distinguish. He loves everyone. Every person born on earth and those born into heaven, he loves us all. He tore himself apart to bring us light and love, not to divide us.

Are politics worth the life of a human being? Does it matter what they wear, what they do, or who they love? Does it matter where they live, which side of a politically drawn border they live on? No. God loves us all, each and every one of us. He may not like how we treat each other, but he loves us anyway.

Action Item:

Stop fighting. Stop blaming. Stop judging (and I say that to myself, too.) Receive God's love in your life. Love God, love everyone. 'Nuff said!

Day 16: 1 Peter 5:7

Give all your worries and cares to God, for he cares about you.

This is such a beautiful verse. Why are we stressing over so many things everyday that in the grand scheme of things matter so little? And I have been (and still occasionally am) Stress Bunny #1.

This verse reminds me of Matthew 11:28 "Then Jesus said, 'Come to me, all you who are weary and carry heavy burdens, and I will give you rest.'"

God loves us. He doesn't want us to be burdened or weighed down by the worries or cares of the world. He wants his best for us, in every area of our lives. It doesn't mean that we won't have troubles; the exact opposite is true, and Jesus said so (see John 16:33). What he does want is for us to bring those cares to him, drop them at his feet and say "Thank you, Lord, for loving me and taking these cares and worries away from me, so I can rest, recuperate, and recharge for the next challenge. Thank you for being my firm foundation, so that when things go wrong, I know I will always have you here beside me, in my corner, cheering me on."

God doesn't want our sacrifices, he wants us to love him, and love everyone else. It's that simple. We don't have to follow thousands of rules. We don't have to perform any rituals or wear certain clothes or say any specific words.

Love God. Love everyone.

Why did he make it this simple for us to follow? Because we'll even mess that up. How many millions of people over the years – at least in the two millennia since Jesus came – have fought wars, abused others, stolen people, land, objects, and all other kinds of atrocities in the name of religion, and even in the name of Christianity? Where does Jesus say anywhere "go kill your neighbour because he's different from you"? Go ahead, look it up. I'll wait.

Give up? Yeah, because it isn't in the Bible anywhere.

People do what we have always done as animal beings: tried to become the alpha of the pack. That is not God's plan for us. He is the Alpha, and we are all his dearly loved children.

Love God, Love everyone. Stop fighting over who is better or who has the most stuff. It. Does. Not. Matter! Any of that only adds to our burdens. We need none of that.

When we choose to love God above all, there is this wash of comfort that flows over us. At least that is what I experience. It's like the love we give him is reflected back over us ten thousand fold. Then when we choose to love everyone else – which will take practice – cares and worries seem to cease. We care less about being number one and more about how we can help others. So then our worries are given over to God, and we're able to help alleviate other's cares and worries, simply by sharing God's love. And so on, and so on. What an encouraging and wonderful world it will be when we finally catch on!

Prayer:

Thank you, Heavenly Father, for always being there for us, for sharing your love, for carrying our worries and burdens. Thank you for taking them from us and bringing us peace. Amen!

Day 17: John 14:27

"I am leaving you with a gift – peace of mind and heart. And the peace I give you is a gift the world cannot give. So don't be troubled or afraid."

It was harder to start writing this morning, because I kept getting lost in this verse. Read it again now, and let it settle into your bones.

My goal in this devotional is to provide encouragement through these Bible verses and what they mean to me. How can I express more encouragement than what these words already provide? How can I interpret what this reading means to me? What does this verse mean to you when you read it?

Jesus' gift to us is this "peace of mind and heart." Calm mind, calm heart. I have spent most of my life as a high-strung stress-bunny living in a cat-like state of readiness for the next thing to possibly happen, whatever that may be. But not these past few years. Has my mind still wandered and gotten distracted? Yes, daily. Have I had moments of stress and anxiety? Have I managed to be calm through it all? Not always, but compared to where I was even five or ten years ago, absolutely!

I can truly say that this peace I feel does not come from worldly things. How do I know? I've tried pretty much all of them. Medication, aromatherapy, counselling. All of these things helped a bit, but they were only calming the symptoms, like putting a bandaid on a gushing wound. The only answer I have for the peace I feel now is that it truly does come from Jesus.

When we started going to church in 2011, I approached it as a child would. I wanted to soak up as much information as I could, learn from our pastor and any guest pastors we had. Whenever we came to a verse like this, talking about the peace the world cannot give, I always felt more calm and reassured than ever before.

Does my mind still race whenever things happen, whether real or "what if" imagined? Yes, but there is this new feeling I have when my mind is going through these ridiculous scenarios. "*Okay, you've let your imagination go out for a walk and get some exercise. Now let it go and rest in me. I've got this.*" That's not a direct quote by any means, but the essence of what I feel like when my mind starts getting frantic. Now I can relax easily into God's word and receive this gift of peace that Jesus has given us all. "Do not be troubled or afraid." What an amazing blessing!

Absolutely take the medication, therapy, counselling and treatment you've been prescribed. Sometimes that is the way Jesus shares his gifts with us. But know that this peace of heart and mind is free to you, available every day, every moment, in all kinds of situations, and whenever you need it. This blessing is free, it is given to all of us, and will be there for us all the days of our lives. What love!

Prayer:

Thank you, Jesus, for this peace of heart and mind that the world cannot give, that you freely gave us. I pray that everyone who reads this and everyone around them receive this amazing blessing into their lives, and rest easy with this peace. In Jesus' name I pray, Amen!

Day 18: Job 22:28

You will succeed in whatever you choose to do, and light will shine on the road ahead of you.

Why don't we all have this plastered on our mirrors so that it is the first thing that we see each morning? This is where we should be focusing our energy — on the statement that we will succeed in whatever we do.

Of course we can succeed — we must believe it and have faith! Why do we give up on ourselves so easily? Why do we give up on our dreams?

Sometimes we give up on them because when we were young we were told to abandon them, that it didn't make any sense, and that dream wouldn't give us enough money to live on.

Probably the greatest example of rejecting this mindset I've ever heard of is from Dom Famularo, a drummer, educator, mentor, and author. When he was young his father told him he should give up his dream of being a drummer and instead choose another job that he didn't like but would be more stable, his response was essentially "so the choice is do what I love and make little money, or do a job I hate and make little money." He chose the career that he loved, and became one of the most influential drum and life educators for decades, influencing thousands of people all over the world with his joyful enthusiasm. Sadly we lost him to cancer in 2023. I highly recommend his book "The Cycle of Self Empowerment."

Why not do what we love? It may take us a while to figure out what it is, but let us follow that light on the road ahead of us, where God is showing us the way. Keep taking tiny steps to reach our dreams.

I have to admit, for most of my life I've avoided my dreams and my gift. I aimlessly worked retail jobs for most of my early 20s. When I went to college I didn't pick a field that I loved, but settled for what I had an affinity for that would lead to a good job. Fast forward over twenty years later, and that decision has secured a good life for me and my husband, and allowed me to explore different artistic expressions, and even live out a childhood dream of participating in an archaeological dig while earning my Anthropology degree. But through it all, I still felt like something was nagging at me. Even when I was focusing more on my art something wasn't right. Then I realized it had been staring me in the face the entire time.

I love writing. I love all kinds of writing. It comes easy to me, and words flow from my mind onto paper so easily, whereas they get all jumbled up when I try to talk aloud. So here I am, stepping into one of my earliest and most persistent loves. Writing. Thank you for coming along for the ride!

Thoughts:

Step into your dreams. Have faith in God to guide you, to show you the way. Do not be afraid, as he's said to us so many times. Trust God, trust Jesus, trust the Holy Spirit, and have faith! And it is NEVER too late to pursue your dreams. Amen!

Day 19: Psalm 37:4

Take delight in the LORD, and he will give you your heart's desire.

I have to admit it, it is often hard to start these devotionals without repeating the verse or simply saying "wow!" Really, the verses alone are enough to inspire and encourage us if we simply sit and soak with them for a while. But that wouldn't make it a very interesting devotional; or would it?

Isn't life like that? We're sailing along day-in and day-out, living our lives, then Wham! Something occurs to us or we're gripped by a sudden realization or inspiration. "Wow! I'm a really good gardener! Why am I going to the office everyday? Why don't I take up landscaping?" or "Hey, I love working with numbers, why don't I pursue accounting?" or "I love architecture — I wonder if I can make the switch and pursue that? Should I start designing eco-friendly homes?"

Or like me. I touched on this a little bit yesterday, that this past year I've been struggling with what I want to be when I grow up. I recently turned fifty and it seemed time to get down to the business of living my dreams instead of working for a living. For so long I've put my dreams on hold to be financially stable and build a life with my husband, who I absolutely adore. It's a very simple modest life in a simple modest home. It is a home full of love and it's ours. But something has always been missing in my life.

In 2018 I decided to set up a website for myself as an artist. I've dabbled in different arts and crafts for years and decided if I had a website I would have to commit to being an artist. I was making pottery most of the time, so I could have said "potter," but that felt too limiting to me. I do lots of arts: pottery, painting, drawing, crochet, sewing, quilting, knitting — all types of art that inspires me. I even sing and write songs for fun. What was one thing I missed on the list that I seemed to most shy away from?

I write.

I never thought of it, because it simply *is* what I do. Whenever the chance to write something for work or school came up, I dove into it. I love the process, the craft of stringing together words to make something beautiful; something concrete pulled out of the ether of imagination. Why was I ignoring something that I was good at, that came easily to me, and that I loved to do? It was like a lightning rod moment that took about three months to realize. Then it finally hit me while I was writing devotionals in the morning: "D'oh! I'm a writer!"

I was taking delight in the Lord, writing about his Word in the Gospels of Matthew, Mark, Luke, and John, when I finally realized I was actually living my heart's desire. So here we are.

Thoughts:

God truly does give us all we ever need in life – sometimes we simply have to pause, breathe, and open our eyes to the gifts he gives us. Even if we can only work on them for fifteen minutes a day. Thank you Heavenly Father! Amen!

Day 20: Mark 4:21

Then Jesus asked them, "Would anyone light a lamp and then put it under a basket or under a bed? Of course not! A lamp is placed on a stand, where its light will shine."

I've always found this verse encouraging. Jesus was talking in parables and explaining them to the disciples, and in verse 23 he reiterated "anyone with ears to hear should listen and understand." That's where it gets a little muddy for me. I've always read this verse as encouragement to let the light that shines inside each of us to shine in the world, and not hide or diminish our gifts.

We never know when something we say or do may be that one thing that helps someone, that brightens their day, that keeps them from doing something negative or harmful. That extra smile, that extra "thank you" or "no, you go ahead," while waiting in line.

There is so much darkness, violence, and negativity in this world. So much hurt, pain, and hopelessness. However, each one of us has a light inside us; a never ending glimmering hope of love and peace inside our soul. Life has often stamped it out so it is down to a tiny glowing ember, the smallest of sparks. All that is needed to reignite it is hope, only a miniscule glimmer of hope. And we can find that hope in Jesus.

I never thought that I would say that. To be perfectly honest, most of my life I actively ran from God, filled with shame for poor decisions I made and things that happened to me. I felt that God was all judgment and punishment; that humans needed atonement for sins, requiring rituals and priests to cleanse us of our sins, all the time while judging us. But I found out that is not God's love at all.

Matthew 11:28 says "Come to me all you who are weary and carry heavy burdens, and I will give you rest." That is Jesus' love. That is God's love through Jesus. He loves us as we are, as pristine or damaged as we may be. He loves us in our brokenness, and sees the best of us, the best of our lives, our heart, and our soul. He knows the dreams we still harbour in our deepest heart of hearts, long locked away behind walls of doubt, negativity, hurt, shame, and the cruelty of this world. Each time we break down one of those walls to let that ember shine a little brighter, we bring more joy, more hope, more happiness and light into the world.

Thoughts:

We cannot let the enemy win in the battle for our spirit, when we know that Jesus has already won it for us. All we have to do is say "yes," believe that we are worthy as God says we are worthy, loved as God says we are loved, and redeemed as God says we are redeemed. Then that tiny ember will start growing, glowing brightly as any sun in our hearts.

Let your light shine! Have faith! Do not be afraid or dismayed, for God has already won. Amen!

Day 21: Deuteronomy 8:18

Remember the LORD your God. He is the one who gives you power to be successful, in order to fulfill the covenant he confirmed to your ancestors with an oath.

I wasn't sure about including all of this verse, because I am only going to focus on the first part, but I wanted to ensure the original context was not lost. Far too often I've seen or heard of people who've cherry-picked parts of Bible verses for their own negative or twisted agendas, and I didn't want to do that here.

I could have simply focused on "he is the one who gives you power to be successful" but I've come to not like those words "power" and "success." Too many people are looking for the wrong kinds of power, and striving for the wrong definition of success. Yes, this is an early quote in the Old Testament, long before Jesus walked the earth.

"Remember the Lord your God." The Old Testament was full of verses telling us to remember God, remember all the commandments and rules, trying to coax humans to stay in line and it didn't work. Miracle after miracle and it would all be lost in people seeking and striving for power and success in their own strength and for their own agenda, not for God.

The only true power is love, plain and simple. God is love, and God loves us. He doesn't want us to be powerful over others, subjugating them to do our will or to our beliefs. At least that's not what I believe. Why would Jesus say the most important commandment was "love God and love your neighbour as yourself" if that was what he wanted? Because we couldn't keep ten rules, he boiled it down to two simple ones: Love God. Love everyone.

Why? Because we're humans. We're easily distracted and on to the next thing. We're easily swayed by other people and their own agendas. We fall prey to those who would make it seem like "the other" is to blame in life, whether that other person looks, loves, or believes differently than we do. We are all the same under these fleshy shells we wear. We are spirit in search of understanding, acceptance, encouragement. In short: LOVE.

God provides all the love in the world, but there is a reason he wanted us to love each other, too. So we could stop trying to be superior to others, to judge others for the life they've been dealt, to hate others because that's what had been handed down in their family or their culture, or to fall prey to wolves in sheep's clothing who say the answer to the problem is to break the spirit of someone else.

Thoughts:

Do not be discouraged because God is with you. God is the source of all power and success, because the truly powerful and the truly successful people know it is not any amount of cash or people under your control, it is the amount of real love in your life that matters. The most important of these is how much love you share through kindness, gentleness, patience, perseverance, peace, charity, joy, encouragement, and faith. Amen!

Wrapping Up:

I hope that the last twenty-one days have been filled with encouragement for you. You may have experienced struggles or some hiccups in life — those always seem to come our way when we are trying to bring more light into our lives — but I hope that this book has been a glimmer of hope or a twinkle of light into what may have been a difficult time.

These are only some of the encouraging verses I found in the Bible. I recommend you explore them on your own, and find other verses that inspire and encourage you. When you do, feel free to share them with me through the contact page on my website www.jackiescottartist.com/contact.

Thank you for taking the time to read my words. I pray that you have received the encouragement that was intended. Amen!

Notes:

A note on the use of he/him/his for God in this book: God made us all humans in his image, male/female, and otherwise. I use he/him/his in this book for consistency rather than interchangeably with they/their or she/her/hers. My intention is not an exclusion of other expressions of genders to use this, but to simplify the phrasing and maintain consistency. Feel free to read she/her/hers or they/theirs wherever he/him/his is written. God knows and loves all his children equally, regardless of human judgment.

Similarly, I have chosen to not capitalize "the enemy" when I refer to evil forces in the world, because I do not wish them to seem more powerful than they think they are.

Resources:

The Cycle of Self Empowerment: Dom Famularo book available online

The Miracle Morning: Hal Elrod
https://miraclemorning.com

Christian Book Academy
https://christianbookacademy.com

Thank You:

Thank you to Lena who once again helped me through the self-editing process, my prayer team partners, the Christian Book Academy community — especially my Progress Pod (go Writing Rockstars!!) — for encouraging me, and my wonderful husband, Michael, for always being by my side (and my biggest cheerleader!) Many blessings to all of you!

Next Steps:

Feel free to follow Jackie on social media at @jackiescott.artist or sign up for her mailing list at www.jackiescottartist.com

Other titles:
30 Days of Joy: A Devotional
30 Days of Joy: A Devotional, Colouring Book and Journal
40 Days of Healing: A Devotional

Forthcoming titles:
Keys to Creativity for Non-Creatives (Spring 2025)

For additional titles, check out Jackie's website

About the Author:

Jackie Scott is a wife, daughter, sister, aunt, cousin, and dearly loved child of God. (Spoiler alert: we are all dearly loved children of God!) Her passion in life is to share God's love with the world through writing and art.

She is also a writer, multi-media and ceramic artist, quilter, knitter, crocheter, and lover of all things craft related. She lives with her husband Michael and their cat Harry in Ontario, Canada.

If you enjoyed this book, please feel free to leave a review on amazon.com or share it with a friend.